T0379376

oasis

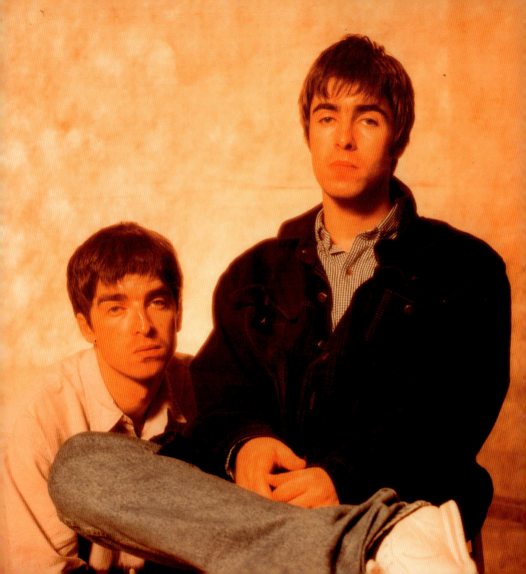

oasis

WHEN ARE YOU GETTING BACK TOGETHER?

15 YEARS OF ANSWERING THE SAME F***ING QUESTION

HARRY MADDISON

SIRIUS

LANGUAGE WARNING:

The quotes contained in this work include language which some people may find offensive.

Page 2: Noel and Liam Gallagher in Japan in 1994.

This edition published in 2025 by Sirius Publishing, a division of
Arcturus Publishing Limited,
26/27 Bickels Yard, 151–153 Bermondsey Street,
London SE1 3HA

Copyright © Arcturus Holdings Limited/Harry Maddison

All rights reserved. No part of this publication may be reproduced, stored in a retrieval system, or transmitted, in any form or by any means, electronic, mechanical, photocopying, recording or otherwise, without prior written permission in accordance with the provisions of the Copyright Act 1956 (as amended). Any person or persons who do any unauthorised act in relation to this publication may be liable to criminal prosecution and civil claims for damages.

ISBN: 978-1-3988-5904-3
AD013107NT

Printed in China

CONTENTS

Introduction 6
2009 9
2010 13
2011 15
2012 23
2013 31
2014 37
2015 41
2016 47
2017 55
2018 67
2019 73
2020 83
2021 89
2022 95
2023 101
2024 115
Epilogue 124
Credits 128

INTRODUCTION

Whatever you think about their music, Liam and Noel Gallagher are two of the most hilarious and quotable rock stars the genre has ever produced, especially when they are slagging *each other* off. Now that the brothers are getting back together, what better time to rake over every hysterical, scornful and (very occasionally) touching thing they have said about each other in response to the dreaded question **'When are Oasis getting back together?'**

For the last 15 years, whichever room Liam and Noel have found themselves in, they've been accompanied by a certain elephant. It is pretty much guaranteed that in the last five minutes of any Gallagher interview between August 2009 and August 2024 a coy journalist has asked 'Man, I love the new single/album/clothing range, so ...
'When are Oasis getting back together?'

Sometimes, the interviewer has tried to be clever and disguise the question – 'Do you miss your brother... when you're out on stage?' Or they've pretended to be concerned for Liam and Noel's mother, Peggy – 'How is your mum coping with her two sons... not getting the band back together?' But, generally, each interviewer has asked the same question that was asked in the interview before, and the interview before that, and the interview before that... ad interview-nitum.

Remarkably, no matter how many times the Gallaghers have been asked 'When are Oasis getting back together?' they've always addressed the question in a frank, funny and fresh way. Their answers range from the angry, cheeky, philosophical, defiant and surreal to the open-hearted, provocative, bitter, catastrophising, vulnerable, cocky, sceptical and totally mental.

The original Oasis line-up in 1993 with (left to right) Paul Arthurs (aka Bonehead), Liam Gallagher, Noel Gallagher, Tony McCarroll and Paul McGuigan.

In the answers that Liam and Noel have given, we can chart the ups and downs of the brothers' professional and personal lives, taking in broken marriages, failed solo projects and the slow thawing of relations between them, from the moment Oasis split to the happy ending of their reunion.

Although, when relations have been bad between the Gallaghers, they have been terrible. There have been years when the brothers couldn't even bear to say each other's name, with Noel referring to Liam as 'the other fella', 'the singer' and 'the tambourine player'. While Liam retitled his brother 'the little fella' and 'potato'. But along with the huge tunes, it's always been the friction that has kept the world enthralled by Oasis.

Over the years, it must have occasionally felt like torture for the Gallaghers. Never mind 'What is Treadstone?' or 'Is it safe?' Imagine *you* fell out horrifically with your brother, with whom you once had a thriving, world-conquering business, and everyone you meet, wherever you go in the world – *everyone* – asks you regardless of what conversation *you* want to have, 'When are you getting back together with your brother?' Now imagine all those conversations in the world are public. The whole world is listening. Fascinated. And what's more, one day someone is going to compile a book of your answers.

This little book is stuffed with the best quotes Noel and Liam have given in response to having the same question whispered, tweeted or shouted at them from scaffolding, for 15 years: **'When are Oasis getting back together?'**

Our story starts in August 2009 when the band broke up but for a bit of context here's what Noel told ITN in July 2009: 'I could never leave Oasis I am Oasis. And I don't think Oasis will ever leave me.'

Let's see what happened next...

2009

When... Barrack Obama became the first African-American president... Swine flu swept the UK... US Airways Flight 1549 crash-landed in the Hudson River... the new digital currency Bitcoin was launched and... Noel Gallagher walked out on Oasis minutes before they were due to headline the Rock en Seine festival near Paris.

Thus began the Gallaghers' purgatory of being asked the same question again and again and again. That question being...

When are Oasis Getting Back Together?

13 November: *Virgin Radio Italia*

Liam

I am as gutted as much as youse are... if I didn't have much to say to him when we were on tour, I've certainly got f*ck all to say to him these days, you know what I mean, so we don't see each other... which is sad but that's life but you know time might... y'know... in a couple of years we might grow up and speak to each other but at the moment we are still very childish.

2 December: *Five/Sky News*

Liam

I think it's done.

Opposite: *Oasis appearing on* Quelli che il calcio *on 19 April 2009 in Milan, in Italy.*

Liam accepts Oasis' award for 'Best Album of 30 Years' on stage at The Brit Awards 16 February 2010 in London.

2010

When... after a volcano erupted in Iceland, dust clouds wrought chaos across Europe... the Deepwater Horizon rig exploded, causing environmental devastation... the first iPad was released... and Liam accepted a Brit award for the Best Album of the Last 30 Years for *(What's the Story) Morning Glory*, thanking Bonehead, Guigsy and Alan White but pointedly not mentioning Noel.

All of which only compounds the clamour....

When are Oasis Getting Back Together?

101.9 RXP (Pinfirled)

Liam
It's a big thing for me and him splitting up, you know what I mean, people can laugh it off and all that tackle but you know it's sad when two family members, whether you are in a band or not, don't get on... but I think we'll speak at some point. I've had enough of him for a bit. I'm sure he feels the same way.

18 July: *The Sunday Times*

Liam
'Don't want to either. It's done and dusted. He's living his life, I'm living mine. I hope he's happy in what he does and I'm happy in what I do.

30 July: *Sky News*

Liam
We won't be back by the end of the year and the only reason Oasis will be come back is when we're f*cking skint. And I'm far from skint as you can tell and I won't be skint for a long long f*cking time believe me, so it ain't gonna be happening.

2011

When... governments were overthrown in the Middle East and North Africa as a consequence of the Arab Spring... Wall Street was occupied by anti-capitalist protestors... Osama bin Laden was shot dead in his compound by US Navy SEALs... and Beady Eye and Noel Gallagher's High Flying Birds released their debut albums.

None of which stopped the Gallaghers from being badgered by the refrain...

When are Oasis getting back together?

John Robb interview

Liam

It'll happen when it happens, you know what I mean, it'll happen, y'know, it's only a year now so I'm not missing him that serious and I don't think he's missing me... I'll probably make the first call and I'll probably get the phone put down but I'm a bigger man, you know what I mean, but it's nowhere near in the future just yet.

LA Weekly

Liam

I'd rather eat my own shit than be in a band with him again.
He's a miserable little f*ck, if you know what I mean.

Mojo Magazine

Liam

It's like wanting your girlfriend back after she's f*cked you off. You'll end up getting yourself ill. They're not going to get me knocking on someone's door saying, 'Come on let's get back together...'. It's done, mate. We had a great time. Beady Eye is where we are now... Get rid of all the Oasis songs and just bathe ourselves in Beady Eye.

Andy Bell, Jeff Wooton and Liam Gallagher of Beady Eye perform on the opening night of their first North American concert tour on 18 June 2011 at the Metro in Chicago, Illinois.

28 February: *The Quietus Magazine*

Liam

I don't feel the need to go round to his f*cking house and have the door slammed in my face. There's no encouragement from any parties whereas, if there was, then it would get sorted. But to get it sorted for what? He wants to go on his own and make his own f*cking music and be the man and let everyone know that he can f*cking flush the toilet without the band or that he can pour his own f*cking tea and that's fine. I haven't got time for that f*cking b*llocks in my life...

...I'll tell you f*cking what, I'm not sitting here for him to go, 'Oh, I'm going to do my solo career and you guys can wait for five years while I f*cking lord it around and have it and then I'll f*cking ring you up if it doesn't go as well as people expect it to be.' F*ck that! We're gone! We're out of here!

19 June: *Shortlist*

Liam

What would be the point? We don't get on with each other. Noel's going down his path and I'm going down mine. No, because the songs we're doing are equally good, I think. It's early days. We only put the album out in February and some of those songs are going to grow into classics. I had a great time singing Oasis songs, without a doubt. But I think Oasis is beatable, man.

8 August: *Rolling Stone Magazine*

Noel

Liam has said that the idea makes him vomit, and it would never happen, so I don't need to add anything to that... I don't need the f*cking money, but I think it's a shame that songs like 'Champagne Supernova,' 'Rock and Roll Star,' 'The Importance of Being Idle,' and 'The Shock of the Lightning' will never be played again in a stadium. That kind of fills me with sadness. The money is kind of irrelevant.

8 October: *The Quietus Magazine*

Noel

Liam's kind of not letting it go. [pause] I'll tell you what really annoys me – when I read about 'the warring brothers'. I'm not at war with anyone. I'm just trying to get on with my f*cking thing. But every time I open a magazine and his head's in it, all I have to do is scan down to the bit where he's calling me a c**t. And if he's supposed to be in the best band in the world, then why the f*ck is he a*sed about me? I mean, just get on with your own thing and leave me be....

14 October: *SKAVLAN SVT NRK, Norwegian Television*

Noel
I haven't seen him for two years.

21 October: *The Jonathan Ross Show, ITV*

Noel
I fear that you're not going to let me go without me saying 'yes'... It would be, it would be nice but we're not together anymore. It's like you don't go on holiday with your ex-wife do you?... I'm not under oath here. I don't have to answer this question. I will straight bat this all night. I can stay here all night.

21 October: *Rolling Stone Magazine*

Liam
If we can put our sh*t aside, we can tour and play the album... [*Morning Glory*]... in its entirety for the 20th anniversary... [Noel's] the one that keeps mentioning it... I want to put him out of his misery. But I think he needs to do his solo thing first and realize he's not that good without his brother. He's got to find out for himself. I'm up for it – I'm not desperate for it. If it doesn't work out, I don't give a sh*t, I'm quite happy with Beady Eye.

25 October: *George Stroumboulopoulos Tonight, CBC Television*

(Liam does a joint interview with his then wife and ex-All Saint, Nicole Appleton, on Canadian TV)

Liam

I'm definitely, well Noel, is the one who started this kind of thing but I'm definitely up for doing a tour. I don't think me and him will ever be in a full-on band again, d'you know what I mean, that's done I think, but Noel was mentioning a tour for the 2015 *(What's the Story) Morning Glory?* [20-year Anniversary] and I think by then, three years, I think I will have grown up a little by then and so will he... If the people want it, who am I to stand in their way? If they don't want it, they don't want it.

9 November: *The Daily Telegraph*

Liam

We're not the only family that's a bit weird. I know lots of brothers and sisters that don't get on... There's not a day goes by when I don't think about Oasis and the music, but it wasn't meant to be... time is a great healer, they say. I'm certainly not putting out an olive branch. Me and our kid are still at loggerheads. I'm not desperate to be in a room with that miserable c**t. Me and him would get into a scrap immediately. But I'd do it for the right reasons, for the music and for the fans. I don't need the f*cking money.

2012

When... the cruise ship, *Costa Concordia*, capsized off the coast of Tuscany... The elementary particle, the Higgs boson, was discovered which revolutionized quantum physics... Queen Elizabeth celebrated her diamond jubilee... and the Gallaghers bumped into each other at a post-London Olympics party where Liam insulted Noel.

Which does nothing to dampen our need to know...

When are Oasis getting back together?

March: *XFM*

Liam (after being voted the Greatest Front Man of All Time)
Me and our kid's relationship is still a bit strange at the moment, so I doubt it.

30 March: *Mark Lawson Talks To...*, *BBC4*

Noel
It won't be the last time I'm ever going to speak to him, of course
I'm going to speak to him again.

It's just done, you know. I'm busy. I'm doing my thing. He's doing his thing.
There's no need to get involved in any of that, at the moment.
Do you know what I mean?

June: *98FM*

Noel

It would be great for everyone else except me... It'd be mega for the millions and millions and for everybody else it would be brilliant, but I wouldn't be very happy about it. I don't think anyone is pushing for a reunion either. Nobody ever brings it up in any seriousness; I mean, Liam does publicly, but he says a lot of things publicly. I wouldn't take anything he says seriously.

Spin.com

Noel

My mam, when I was three, could put an end to a family feud pretty quick. When you're forty-odd and got three kids it's kinda, like, y'know, we'll get on with it if you don't mind.

12 September: *BBC Radio Nottingham*

Noel

He did insult me at a party the other night, so I guess there's been a slight thawing of the ice, yeah. That's the first time he's insulted me since the day I left the band... What can I say? He tried to sue me, y'know what I mean, I don't take that lightly... It went to the steps of the high court then he decided to change his mind.

12 September: *NME*

Noel

Not even if all the starving children in the world depended on it. I know it's the done thing these days and what people do, but it's not what I do. I know bands reform and 'They're bigger than they ever were' and 'They're more successful than they ever were', but Oasis were one of the biggest bands in the world. At any given time, we were one of the five biggest bands in the world. We were the biggest thing to come out of England in 35 years. Why would we do it? For the fans? Nobody ever gave a sh*t about the fans in that band. It's done.'

Opposite: *Liam greets fans on his 40th birthday on 21 September 2012 in London.*

9 October: *The Meaning of Life with Gay Byrne, RTE One*

Noel

Well, this Christmas just gone, she [Peggy] said, 'Call, I've told him to call you and I'm telling you to call him so it's about time you spoke,' and we exchanged texts on Christmas Day. And stuff like that. Liam doesn't have a phone cos he's always losing them, so you've gotta, you've gotta text his missus' phone.

...I'm not that kind of person to be quite honest. I'm not really, I'm not wistful and I don't, I'm not nostalgic and, y'know, if I hear Oasis songs on the radio, I don't think like, 'Oh, God wouldn't that be great.' Evidently, it would be great. But y'know, I'm always one for moving onwards.

24 October: *AV Club*

Noel

Honest to God, it was about six weeks after I left people were saying, 'Do you think you'll ever get back together?' I was like, 'I haven't even made a f*cking record!' It's like, f*ck me! It cost me about a half a million f*cking dollars to get out of that band, and then people were saying, 'When are you going back on tour?' I was like, 'What the f*ck?'

...It's just one of those things, you know? I don't mind. It depends what the question is, really. The reunion thing is a bit of a pain in the a*se. It's like, 'For f*ck's sake.' What else do people want to know about you? I don't know. I don't mind. Ask me a question. I don't tell any lies.

December: The *Evening Standard*

Noel

If the Stone Roses can do it, then anyone can do it. I can understand the man in the street thinking, 'That was such a huge thing, how can you walk away from it?' I understand. When the Sex Pistols reformed, I thought it was the greatest thing of all time. You can never predict what you'll be doing in 20 years' time, but I guess if everyone remains vaguely slim and has not gone bald, then it's on the cards forever.

2013

When... the Boston Marathon was shaken by a terrorist bomb attack... Pope Francis became the new Pope... Edward Snowden leaked evidence that the American authorities were wiretapping the public... and Beady Eye released their second album, *BE*.

Inevitably, the question on everyone's lips was...

When are Oasis getting back together?

15 March: *Time Out Dubai*

Noel

For the sake of headlines all over the press, I'm not going to answer that because it would just be nonsense. Look, it's not going to happen in 2015 [the 20th anniversary of *(What's the Story) Morning Glory?*] because the boys in the other band [Beady Eye] are all flat out busy, they're making a record at the minute so they're going to be on the road until 2015 you'd imagine… That's not to say it won't happen in 25 years time, or 20 years… I understand people are interested, and the Stone Roses have done it, and Led Zeppelin have done it, and blah, blah, blah.

11 April: *Shortlist*

Liam recalls meeting Noel at the post-Olympics party.

Liam

I thought I was pretty pleasant; you know what I mean? I said, 'What do you make of that then, you f*cker?' And he went, 'Uh, yeah, it was alright'. Then I said, 'I seen your mates there, they said to say hello,' and he went, 'Who?' and I said, 'Take That' and he went, 'Urgggh'. That was it and I turned me back and had a drink and then everyone was going ''Ere you are, speak to him' and I said, 'Nope, I'm having a f*cking drink,' and that was it.

Noel and Damon Albarn at the BRIT Awards at The O₂, on 20 February 2013 in London.

31 May: *The Quietus Magazine*

Liam
He's doing his thing and I'm doing mine and it's all good, man. My mam's not crying into her f*cking cup of tea and lemon meringue. She don't give a f*ck. She's hard; she goes, 'You're a d*ck, he's a d*ck. Who shall I go and see this week?'

June: *NME*

Liam
There's unfinished business there. People ask, would I get Oasis back together? I'd do it for nowt, but if someone's going to drop a load of f*cking money, I'd do it for that too. I don't think we'd ever make another record. I doubt we'll ever get back together... We could bury the hatchet for a quick lap of honour.

24 June: *BBC Radio 5*

Liam

We'll see, these things will have to be talked about, but I'm not interested in the f*cking slightest right now... It's not like Noel's knocking at my door with a f*cking box of chocolates and a bunch of flowers going 'Come and speak to me,' and I'm going 'No!' We're just not getting on at the moment.... He's still a f*cking idiot, you know what I mean, and I'm still an idiot to him and all that, but that's life... that's just us joking, y'know, f*cking, that's just how we speak... I don't wish him any bad luck... We didn't get a round of applause when we were together for 18 years so why would everyone worry now we're not going for four years. We lived together for 30 of them years, where were the medals then and the TV programmes then?

20 June: *5 News (ITN)*

Liam

I don't know, man. Me and our kid haven't spoken since 2009, so who knows, man? If it's meant to be, it's meant to be. I'll do it if people want to do it. And I won't do it if people don't want to do it. It's no skin off my nose. I don't go to bed licking Oasis posters and playing Oasis records....

November: *Rolling Stone Magazine*

Noel

We are split up. You've heard that, haven't you? You must've heard... Yeah, so, ergo, band splits up, band is no more. There is no band. So, no, I won't be getting involved. Anyway, if there is a reunion, I won't be in it.

2014

When... the Ebola virus became an epidemic in Africa...The Russians annexed Crimea... Malaysian Airplane Flight 370 mysteriously disappeared from the skies... Liam announceed Beady Eye had disbanded and bookmakers stopped taking bets on whether Oasis would reform for Glastonbury.

Which led the whole world to enquire...

When are Oasis getting back together?

28 April: *TalkSPORT*

Noel

I was in the newsagent the other day when the story broke and there was a thing on the cover of the *Daily Star* that said we were getting five hundred million to come back, which is half a billion right? Half a billion!... If anyone's out there listening, I'll do it for half a billion of anything... milk bottle tops, pot noodles, crisps, Yorkshire teabags, condoms even. I'd do it for half a billion condoms!

17 November: *The Christian O'Connell Breakfast Show, Absolute Radio*

Noel

Will we [Oasis] be playing Glastonbury next year? Yes, we will and we are getting back together, I think it's going to be on a Thursday. I think it's going to be February the sixteenth at twenty past five... Because, quite frankly, the more I say 'no', the more these stories, these stories go on. But if I just say 'yes', maybe they'll think, 'Oh you're taking the mickey, aren't you?' Ummm, the answer to that is 'No!'

Opposite: *Noel performs with Johnny Marr at Brixton Academy on 23 October 2014 in London.*

21 November: *XFM Breakfast show with John Holmes*

Jon Holmes quotes Dave Grohl who said he'd only play Glastonbury 2015 if Prince and a reformed Oasis played too.

Noel
I'm available that weekend, I'm available that weekend. It's not up to me though, is it?

22 November: *The Jonathan Ross Show, ITV*

Noel
I don't see the appeal. I don't see it. If I close my eyes I don't see it happening. That's not to say that it never will but I've got a lot of things going on...There's no problem. Because we don't speak to each other, there's no problem.

2015

When... the Paris Agreement was signed by world leaders in an effort to combat climate change... and dogged by corruption allegations, FIFA president Sepp Blatter resigned... the first images of Pluto were taken by the New Horizons space probe... and Noel Gallagher's High Flying Birds released their second album, *Chasing Yesterday*.

But people were as keen as ever to know...

When are Oasis getting back together?

16 January: *NME Magazine*

Noel

Paul Weller threatens me that if I ever go back in Oasis, that'll be it between us. He's always says 'You f*cking heard all these f*cking things about your f*cking reunion?' and I'm like 'Yeah, I know' and he goes 'You're not f*cking doing it?' and I'm like 'No', and he's going 'Good good good'. Basically, if Oasis ever did get back together, which is highly unlikely, I'd have to leave London and move back to Manchester. Because he'd put my windows in.

January: *Q Magazine*

Noel

If I was ever going to do it, it would only be for the money. This isn't me putting it out there, by the way. Would I do it for charity? No way. We're not that kind of people. For Glastonbury? I don't think [organizer] Michael Eavis has got enough money. But would we get back together one day? As long as everybody is still alive and still has their hair, it's always a possibility. But only for the money.

...I think it's ingrained in the English psyche — this idea that the glory days, the Empire, are behind us... Led Zeppelin! The Smiths! The Jam! They should all reform! Why? So, a load of middle-aged people can stand in the O_2 and go, 'They're not as good as they used to be.' It'd be the same with Oasis.

14 February: *The Daily Telegraph*

Noel

We texted on Christmas Day. Something to do with Bing Crosby. Yeah, I never realised how ludicrous that 'Little Drummer Boy' song was with David Bowie... But Liam's got to clear the decks, sort his sh*t out and start again. I don't know what he'll do. I can't speak for him.

19 March: *Rockpalast, WDR Germany*

Noel

Yeah, half a billion pounds. That what it's gonna take, that's what it's gonna take, but I'd even take, I might take dollars. Half a billion though something, not lira though; that's f*cking worthless. That's what it's gonna take. That's 500 million. That's a lot of money. And even then, I might think twice about it because the last time I went on tour with Oasis its wasn't very good – ha ha ha hmmm.

20 April: *Pete Mitchell interview for Absolute Radio*

Noel

It won't be happening…. What people don't understand is that for them it would be one night and it would be clearly be amazing for them but for the people in the band it would be like a full year.

1 May: *Huff Post Live*

Noel

I can only say what I've already said a thousand times. It isn't gonna happen. And if it is gonna happen, I won't be doing it, but it's a shame that these 'mystery sources' keep getting the hopes of the fans up. Y'know the last thing was that me and Liam had a gentlemen's agreement. And the mystery source is a source very close to Liam. And I'm sure that he wakes up with her every morning. And they should cease from that cos everybody who is anyway involved with that band knows where it all sits and it isn't gonna happen and it isn't likely to happen.

…We were never that kind of family all sitting around a dinner table at Christmas with party hats on going 'Wahay, you're great', 'No but you're better', 'No but you're better than I am', 'No, but you are gorgeous'. No, there's none of that going on, erm, we're just quite a dysfunctional mob unfortunately.

Noel and High Flying Birds perform at the Mitsubishi Electric Halle in Düsseldorf, in Germany in March 2015.

September: *Chris Moyles Show, Radio X*

Noel
Well, one should never say never, should one look like a bit of an idiot somewhere down the road, when you're waving a cheque for a quarter of a billion in *The Sun*!

November: *Esquire Magazine*

Noel
If I'd thought there was anything left to achieve, I wouldn't have left Oasis. I made a very snap decision in the car that night in Paris: we've done it all, we're only going to go round in circles now and do bigger tours and make more money and get another f*cking drummer – we'd had about 11 drummers at that point... You name it, we did it all.

Ten years from now, if I wake up one morning and go, 'You know what? I think I'm going to do it,' I can guarantee you, just for spite, Liam would say, 'Oh, no, I'm not keen.' Because that's the way sh*t works.

2016

When... Donald Trump was elected President of the USA... the World Health Organization announced an outbreak of the Zika virus... the UK voted to leave the EU... and Liam started tweeting that his brother looked like a potato.

Now the universe is insistent...

When are Oasis getting back together?

15 March: *El Pais , Uruguay SI*

Noel
I do feel sometimes it would be easier to be in a band. Not necessarily *that* band.

11 July: *Rolling Stone Radio*

Noel
...Shall we start another rumour? We could start a rumour I'm going to do it without Liam and I'm going to use a hologram like they did with Tupac at Coachella.

19 September: *Rolling Stone Magazine*

Noel
[I'm asked] every day of the week...People say, 'You'll definitely re-form — you will,' and I'm just like, 'That's so f*cking rude.' They try to Jedi-mind-trick me.

28 March: *The Australian*

Noel
There's is always a chance it could happen for the money and there's nothing wrong with that because money is amazing. I don't know whether you have any. Do you have any? It's f*cking good to have a shitload, trust me... when I close my eyes I don't see it happening.

August: *Q Magazine*

Liam
I believe Oasis will sail again and it'll be glorious. If it's really about the fans, Noel, let's do it – because they want it. One year. Tour for a year. We'd smash it. My bags are still packed from my last tour, so I'm ready... D'you think I want to be in a band with that c**t? He says, 'Liam has to change.' Get to f*ck... If the guy doesn't want me back in our band, then I don't want to either... I don't want to be in a band with someone who doesn't want me. Every f*cking soundcheck he'd stand in the middle and sing. The geezer's got small-man syndrome... Noel lives in a £17-million house. That changes you, I reckon. You have appropriate furniture, appropriate kitchens, appropriate red wine that Bono's recommended. And Damon Albarn becomes your mate. Fair dos, but not for me.

17 October: *MCFC City TV, SI*

Liam

I'm not bored with the question, I think it's good that people still care, d'you know what I mean. I think I said it's down to Noel, isn't it? If people stop asking him, I think he'll get it back together... it's like little man syndrome... they get the power don't they, so, like when you're that little and you get the power you're just buzzing going 'No, not today', know what I mean?

...Stop asking the little man, then he'll get the a*se and think no one loves him anymore and then he'll probably do something about it.

Opposite: *Noel and High Flying Birds perform at Latitude Festival at Henham Park on 19 July 2015 in the UK.*

1 October: *Daily Telegraph*

Liam

Anyway, his missus... won't let him get that band back together. She wears the trousers, mate. The olive branch has been put out many times, and he's blanked it. It's a shame we can't bury the hatchet, but it's not like I'm messing with the brakes on his car, or he's putting my windows through. It's just banter, isn't it, until one of us grows up.

...It *is* a shame. I don't see his kids, he doesn't see my kids, and it hurts my mum, and all that tackle... It's all very childish and ridiculous, but there you go. I'm quite enjoying it, actually.

..So yeah, here we are now, 20 years later, bored out of our f*cking minds. The party is well and truly over!... I'd love to, but obviously – it's down to Ronnie Corbett, innit.

2 October: *Supersonic Premiere, Sky News*

Liam

But there'll be no cap in the hand and no banjo, you know what I mean? A little f*cking skinny, stringy dog outside his house going 'Please sir, I need a f*cking band, mate.' If it happens, it happens. If it doesn't, it f*cking doesn't, we move on.

2 October: *Supersonic Q&A with Liam Gallagher and the director*

Liam

No I haven't spoken to him, mate, but y'know, you knows the score, everyone knows me and him are cool. Well, we're not cool, actually. Well, I'm f*cking cool and he ain't cool but we will be cool at some point.

October: *Johnny Vaughan, XFM*

Liam

I mean it's like, I'm here, I'm ready to go. I mean our kid bangs on as if I've done … as if I f*cking stabbed his cat or something… Like if people think by me having a dig on Twitter is stopping the band [getting] together like, you're f*cking off your heads like, yeah? The reason why the band ain't getting back together is cos Noel needs to be surrounded by 'yes' men, yeah. And I ain't one, right!

2017

When... after the terrorist attack at Manchester Arena, Liam performed at 'One Love Manchester'... and Noel and his band headlined 'We Are Manchester', a benefit concert to mark the reopening of the Arena, donating the proceeds of 'Don't Look Back in Anger' to a Manchester charity. However, despite both brothers supporting their hometown, their feuding in the media became ever more vicious.

Which led many to believe it was futile even to ask...

When are Oasis getting back together?

1 June: *Channel 4 News*

Liam

I don't think he wants it, man, you know what I mean; he's quite happy in his solo world... All these people going 'I wish you'd get back together'. I'm ready to go, man. So it's all down to him and I'm not putting the blame on him, but he's the one who doesn't want it.... I've got kids and when they argue and they're not getting on and stuff you feel the pain, man, y'know.

4 June: *The Observer*

Liam

No. It ain't happening, mate. When I think about it, being in a band with him bores the death out of me. He's changed, as a person. He's not someone I want to be in a band with. He's part of the establishment... Oasis have got no unfinished business.

13 June: *Pinkpop, Toazted*

Liam

I've said before I've got no problem with our kid. I don't mind getting back together, he doesn't want to do it, what can I do? I can't f*cking force him. If he turned around to me and said, 'Listen we're getting back together,' I'd be like, 'Cool, what's the set list?'

...I wish I was still in the band singing songs to them beautiful people with the band members but there's nothing I can do about it. The ball is in Noel Gallagher's court, Noel Gallagher. Not mine.

31 July: *Howard Stern Show, Sirius FM*

Liam

When we start liking each other, inevitably, I think the next step would be to take the band out for a little spin around the block... I love Oasis. It's the best thing ever... I love my brother. We're just going through a little dodgy patch at the moment... I just see a potato.

Liam Gallagher performs on stage during the One Love Manchester Benefit Concert at Old Trafford Cricket Ground on 4 June 2017 in Manchester, in the UK.

7 August: *Chris Moyles XFM*

Liam

If we're just doing it for the money then I ain't doing it, d'you know what I mean, and listen it would be nice to have a hundred million pound in your f*cking bank account... but I've had a hundred million pound so it would have to be a little bit more... It's about me and him. If me and him get back together as mates and as brothers and all that tackle, then it'll naturally happen, but at the moment it's a f*cking bazillion light years away, man.

October: *Q Magazine*

Noel

I've been very consistent about it. I don't need the money, I don't need the glory, I don't need to relive the memories. If I was to get Oasis back together tomorrow and then do a tour, I'd have a hundred million dollars in the bank but I'd have learnt f*ck all. It would be the death of me as a person.

...I'll be in a boozer and someone will say, 'F*cking hell, our kid's gone all like Donald Trump, but y'know, I'm trying to soar like an eagle, an eagle, and I'm being asked to comment on the ramblings of a common pigeon.

October: *Clint Boon, XS Manchester*

Liam

I do I f*cking love him and I wish we were still in Oasis... and regardless of that I wish we were still mates and that, but it is what it is... There is nothing more I would love than to have his head in my arm in a good firm headlock and me just go like that (SLAP SLAP SLAP) on his wig.... He knows deep down that I love him, and whatever he thinks I did, I didn't and if I did do it, I didn't mean it, so there you go.

8 October: *A conversation with Liam Gallagher, Bandwagon*

Liam

Well, it just goes to show how f*cking boring everybody else is and how sad these so called rock'n'roll bands out there [are] if they're still looking at fifty-year-old men to get back together... I get why people want it. Different generations that never got to see us, and while we're still alive why not make it happen, you know what I mean. There are no conditions, I sing the songs, you sland over there.

9 October: *Music Week*

Liam

I think... one day man. I'm not sure when, but I think it will do because I know how people with egos work. Once they get a bit dented, their heads go, you know what I mean? One day our kid will slowly start coming down to earth. It's all in his hands – as soon as he gets a bit of a whack or things aren't going too well, he'll roll out the Oasis cards, without a doubt. So, I'd love it, man, but I'm certainly not sat outside his house with a box of chocolates and violins going, 'Please, please'.

17 October: *Bilingual podcast, Episode 74*

Noel

No, no, no, no, no. It's done. OK, let me explain. Are you two married? OK, so let's just say you have an epic f*cking fallout and your relationship ends. One of you slightly goes insane and is publicly behaving like a moron, right? Now would you go on holiday with that person again? Well, there you go then, there's your answer.

18 October: *Q Awards, Absolute Radio*

Liam

Oasis ain't getting back together, there you go, but The Verve might be and The Stone Roses might be... I think it's a real waste, y'know what I mean, when people sit there going, 'Well how much is he getting? Oh I dunno and how big is his dressing room?'

...The f*cking Verve, The Stone Roses, we shouldn't have to wait for these things till when we're in heaven or wherever we go. We're living on Earth, man, let's f*cking do it now! You know what I mean? But that's just wishful thinking.

29 November: *Q 104.3 Out of the Box podcast,*

HOST: *What will happen first a Smiths reunion, an Oasis reunion or the Second Coming?*

Noel

The Second Coming, I would have thought. I wouldn't have thought there'll be a Smiths reunion. And I know for a fact there won't be an Oasis reunion. So, I'm afraid the Second Coming of the Lord is what you've all got to look forward to.

15 November: *The Independent*

Liam

I don't hold grudges me... But it's not happening... Even when we were in Oasis, I'd come out of interviews and that c**t would slag me off. I'd go in to do my bit and the geezer [interviewer] would turn round and say: 'F*cking hell, he don't like you, does he?' So what if Noel's getting a hard time. I'm just letting people know how much of a c**t he is.

I love my brother, the geezer I used to be in a band with – I f*cking adore him. Now he's like guy smiley, he's mister f*cking happy, I just look at him and I just go 'f*ck off', that ain't the brother I know. But the one I was in a band with, having a beer and a laugh with, without a doubt I adore him. But people do change, some for the better – some for the worse.

16 November: *Front Row, Radio 4*
(Interview with Stig Abell)

Noel
I will never walk the stage with that band again. There's many reasons, there's loads of reasons. It used to be professional, right? Professional reasons like I don't want to do it, I did it. Why taint the legacy? But now it's personal, y'know… people are coming after my family and one particular person has legitimised it and for that reason you've seen the last of Oasis.

29 November: *Nihal Afternoon Edition, BBC Radio 5 Live*

Noel
He's a filthy little narcissist and I have no time for people like that... the thing about Oasis was it was all about the struggle and the power trips within the band and on the night that I left I made a conscious decision – why am I in this band that is making me so unhappy? I'll just go and do something else. On the night that I quit and it was in Paris, I was like anything is better than this.

Doing what I do now is so fluid. I've got three girls in the band who are coming on tour with me and they're not backing singers, they are actually in the band. You couldn't do that in Oasis, you'd have to have a meeting, y'know [Noel impersonates Liam] 'Birds, in the band? I don't know, mate, it's not rock'n'roll, is it?'

14 December: *The One Show, BBC 1*

Noel
I'm gonna say no... [Hosts and crew SIGH] We can say yes. Shall we say yes? Let's do it again and say yes... Absolutely, I would be thrilled to do it.

24 December: *Radio 6 Music, BBC Sounds*

Liam

I don't think we should have broke up, y'know what I mean. Everyone could have gone off and do[ne] their thing. Whether Bonehead wants to be a ventriloquist or, well, he weren't in the band at the time or I want to go and y'know play tennis or whatever....

...At least, it happened. It's a shame that it ended like that but that's the way it is... At the end of the day, I've got an album coming out. He's got an album coming out. The Gallagher brothers are doing some good stuff at the moment. Oasis ain't happening, the second best thing is two solo albums, I s'pose.

2018

When... the Camp Fire becomes the most destructive wildfire in California's history... Elon Musk launched the Tesla Roadster into space... a children's football team was rescued from the Tham Luang caves... the South Korean President, Moon Jae-in, met North Korea's Supreme Leader, Kim Jong Un,... and Liam and Noel toured the world, separately.

Which only drove people to demand...

When are Oasis getting back together?

10 January: *The Project, Australia*

Liam

Didn't catch up with him over Christmas, didn't catch up with him over last Christmas, not caught up with him over Christmas for about 15 years. He goes to see me mam and we sort of share me mam. I'll have her next Christmas, but yeah, no, the truth is he's said a few things that I didn't like and I've let him have it again, so that's the way it goes. 'Cos he thinks his sh*t don't stink, you know what I mean… I'm watching him.

10 January: *9 News, Australia*

Liam

Hey listen I'd love to, man… I think Noel and his merry men they got their little world, d'you know what I mean… and I've got my world with my mates and my girlfriend and I think for us to get back together, he's got to give up half of that, y'know what I mean? So I think he's a bit of a control freak, so I don't think that'll happen because he likes to be the main man, and when he's next to me he doesn't get a look in.

January: *Q Magazine*

Liam

He's not allowed to, his missus won't let him now. 'Cos she's another one. I know for a fact, deep down, he wants to be playing stadiums.... You can only play stadiums when I'm there.

16 February: *NME*

In late 2017, Liam put out a series of Tweets suggesting he and Noel were on good terms, seeing each other over Christmas and had called a truce. Jordan Bassett asked whether Liam had a real truce with Noel over Christmas?

Liam

Well in my head I did. Well, it is Christmas and my mam's always going, 'Look, you know, calm down,' and all that and I sort of had a couple of drinks and I thought, 'Yeah, I'll just put it out there,' but that's not happening is it... It was just a blag, man. Just me drunk... I'm sorry if I'm breaking people's hearts; it was just a little drunken thing and that's the way it is. You should know me by now.

23 February: *The Chris Moyles Show, Radio X*

Liam
We're not getting back together and I haven't seen our kid before you ask.

March: *Chris Evans Breakfast Show, BBC Radio 2*

Liam
The man from Del Monte. He say 'yes'.

16 April: *It's Electric with Lars Ulrich, Apple Music*

Noel
I'm really really happy about what we did in the past, but I'm really f*cking happy about where I am now. It's so calm and you can, y'know, you can get three girls in the band and take them on the road and that's it... You've only got to please yourself. So, I'm really really pleased with where I am now.

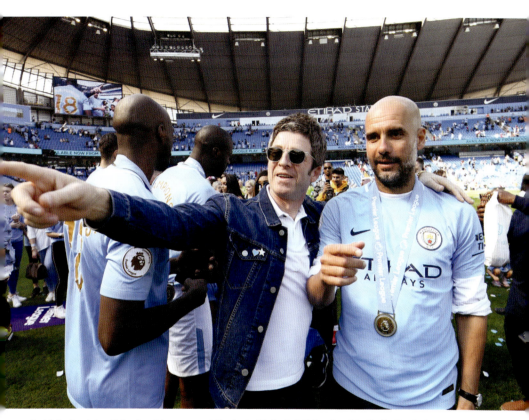

Noel Gallagher chats with Pep Guardiola, manager of Manchester City Football Club on the pitch after the Premier League match between Manchester City and Huddersfield Town at the Etihad Stadium on 6 May 2018 in Manchester, in the UK.

June: 'Stop the Cocks', Daily Star

Liam

I think Oasis is over...I actually don't think Oasis would have him, let alone him have Oasis. He'd only want to get some girl in playing scissors at the back or someone f*cking eating candy floss.'

December: 'Dig Out Your Singer', Mojo

Noel

He got his thing now - which is effectively my thing - and when he's headlining Finsbury Park I'm sat there watching *Match of the Day* getting a PRS cheque for him playing my songs. But instead of making him happy, it's made him worse. It's made him even angrier (laughs).

Liam wants to do it for his ego – he never gave a shit about the fans. He wouldn't have walked off stage 25 times in his career if he gave a shit about the fans.

2019

When ... the American House of Representatives voted to impeach Donald Trump... protests in Hong Kong turned into riots... the cathedral of Notre-Dame in Paris was engulfed in flames... the Event Horizon Telescope captured an image of a black hole for the first time... and Noel's wife, Sara, called Liam a 'fat tw*t' on Instagram.

Which does f*ck-all to stop people asking...

When are Oasis getting back together?

2 May: *Johnny Vaughan, Radio X*

Noel

Well, when bands break up, they break up for a reason. And when they get back together, it's usually that reason rears its head not soon after... You get me an Adidas holdall with eight million quid in it, I'm there.

June: *BBC Breakfast News, BBC*

Liam

I don't want the band to get back together. We shouldn't have split up, y'know what I mean. He's making out as if I've stabbed one of his cats, or y'know slapped one of his kids or, dare I say it, tried it on with his missus.... It's like leave it out, mate.

10 June: *Chris Moyles Show, XFM*

Liam

I hope wherever he is in the world, he's sat in a dark room with his head in his hands, in shame.

16 June: *The Sunday Times*

Liam
Even if I hate him, I miss him at the same time. I miss what we had.

Late Night with Seth Meyers

Noel
Are you asking me? No. It's an ongoing thing, it's like people say, 'I have to ask you', you don't have to ask. When people say like an Italian guy (Italian accent), 'Tell me No-el will there be an Oasis reunion?' I say, 'I sincerely hope not.'

5 August: *The Guardian*

Noel
It boils down to, on a personal level, f*ck him. But also, artistically, why do it again? You know, I was watching the news the other night and he was on there, threatening to break my jaw – live on the ITV news! Isn't there a law against that? – and it's about an Oasis reunion and he's like: 'Me bags are packed, mate.' And I'm thinking: 'Who are you expecting to call you? Me?' Nobody wants to be in a band with him apart from a load of indie Championship players – journeymen, who are in it for all the crisps they can eat.

Liam performs at the 2019 Glastonbury Festival on 29 June 2019 in the UK.

14 September: *The Daily Telegraph*

Liam

No. F*ck 'im. F*ck it being fixed. I'm quite happy doing this now, 'cause I don't have to see that miserable little c**t with his little Simon Cowell Cuban heels that give him a high-rise.

17 September: *BBC Radio 5 Live with Nihal Arthanayake*

Liam

It's down to him and it's down to the people around him. There's only so much, so many like olive branches you can give someone, you know what I mean, without sort of going 'actually I don't think he really cares anymore', but that's life. We'll see how it ends up.

...I was saying the other day, I was saying 'Look, God forbid something happens to my mam'... and we haven't made up by then. There will be war, you know what I mean... Obviously, I say sh*t in the press and he says stuff and his missus says summat and I say summat and all that, and it's all childish and we should all grow up and all that. At the end of the day, basically, it's down to him, innit. You know what I mean?

2 September: *The Jonathan Ross Show, ITV*

Liam

I don't know what it is with him at the moment... I don't now why we split up. I'd like to know... maybe I might have been a bit too rock'n'roll for him and that, I might have cancelled a few gigs and that. I might have stayed up later than I should have some nights, but we're not S f*cking Club Seven.

(Ross asks if Liam's song 'One of Us' is about Noel)

What are the lyrics? 'Get the band back together you w*nker'?

12 September: *Vanity Fair, Italy*

Noel

When people ask me about the Oasis reunion, I often feel the only person on Earth to ask: but what for? Why try to recreate the perfect cake? It would be stupid! That night in Paris I made a very quick decision, I spent less than a minute on it. The whole history of Oasis flashed in front of my eyes, and I asked myself: what else do we want? More tours? No. More money? I already have more than enough. I know why Liam would want a reunion. He's ashamed of what he's done and would like to correct his mistakes. All those concerts, especially in Italy, when he left the stage as if nothing had happened in front of 70,000 people... He needs to think about this first.

13 October: *Today, Australia*

Noel

It's not for me... it would have to be some extraordinary circumstances that brought me and Liam back together... I'm not saying those extraordinary circumstances don't exist, but if I close my eyes and look into the future, I don't see it but... Who knows? I mean, I know better than anyone. Yeah, maybe you should never say never... but....

21 October: *Interview, BMI London Awards*

Noel

Now we're doing our separate things. Well, he's doing my thing and I'm doing my thing too. I don't ever think about it, I genuinely don't ever think about it. I know we live in an age of nostalgia. And everyone wants to get back together and all that, but I genuinely don't think about it. I only ever think about it when I'm asked about Oasis... It never dawns on me that, oh well maybe. There's always an anniversary coming up in the music business. There'll be one tomorrow morning for, y'know, Bonehead's hair falling out – 'Oh I wish they'd get back together and do a benefit gig for his f*cking nose hair' or summat.

21 October: *Music Week*

Noel

I mean, if you're skint, do it. Don't lie about it though, just say you're doing it for the f*cking money! Money's all right, it's not a dirty thing. I *love* making money – the more I've got of it, the better. I guess it's a personal thing: I don't need the money; I don't need the hassle; I don't want to put the High Flying Birds on hold for two years to go around the world arguing with someone I don't get on with, what's the point in doing that? So it doesn't appeal to me. If I ever lose all my money investing in f*cking arms dealing somewhere in Chechnya and I'm skint, trust me, I'll be the first at the press conference. But I won't be lying about it, I'll say I'm doing it for the f*cking money.

22 October: *Flood*

Liam
There's no reconnecting with him. That geezer's on another planet.

October: *Associated Press*

Liam

Yeah, I wish so. Only for the brother side of it. Not a bit about Oasis. The most important thing is about me and him being brothers. I've got another brother who he doesn't speak to. It would be nice if all three of us would be together... I mean, I didn't kick his cat. I didn't try hugging up with his Mrs or anything like that. I don't know what his problem is.

November: *Forbes Magazine*

Liam

If it happens, it happens. It'd be nice. Me mom would like to see us on stage again. I'd much prefer to be a brother with my brother than to go around touring with him, hating each other and just cutting the coin. I wouldn't do that. F*ck that.

19 November: *Beats 1 with Zane Lowe, Apple Music*

Noel

Can I stop you there? That doesn't mean sh*t to me. Because he's on f*cking Twitter right now, saying the exact opposite. If he's in here, on camera, playing to the gallery, fine, good. Actually, when it f*cking matters, when he's abusing my wife and my kids, it's like no no no no no, you don't get to f*cking do both, do you know what I mean? Either be a c**t and own it, right, or don't be a c**t... When I eventually see him, he'll realise it's not f*cking banter.

December: *The Monthly, Schwartz Media*

Liam

He's just going through a funny phase, and he's surrounded by a lot of f*cking idiots and they need to shake their heads as well. Shame on them. They should be more trying to get Noel and me back together, a lot more. Not as a band, they should just be more encouraging. Me and him together are a force; separated we're a lesser force. So it's good for some people, whoever they are, that we're separated and at loggerheads. But it's a shame that me mum has to witness it.

2020

When... the COVID-19 pandemic led to a worldwide lockdown that engendered chronic social isolation and the biggest economic recession since the Great Depression of the 1930s... George Floyd was killed by a white policeman in Minneapolis... armed forces overthrew the government of Mali... and Liam sang various Oasis hits with reworked lyrics to get his fans to wash their hands.

All of which begged the inquiry...

When are Oasis getting back together?

7 February: Rolling Stone Magazine

Liam

And I'm not desperate. I'm not desperate about anything. A lot of people, say, 'Oh, he's desperate.' I don't give a sh*t. I'm quite happy to be doing this. We should never have split up, you know what I mean? So that's people thinking that I'm desperate to get the band back, and that's not true… It'll be 50/50, and I'll be choosing who's in the band as well, because if he thinks I'm joining the High Flying Birds but calling it Oasis, he's got another thing coming. Bonehead will be in the band and we'll be ripping it up, man.

…But if we do it without becoming mates again, I think it would be a f*cking waste of time. I don't think we'd last the first chorus of f*cking 'Rock 'n' Roll Star.' I think I'd end up sticking it on him.

28 February: *NME*

Liam

The geezer's ego's out of control. Let me tell you this: it has been offered and he knows about it. He's obviously gonna say no, because he'd like to be the person to break the news to people because he's the f*cking oracle. And obviously I'm his little brother, who's doing well and I'm here to spoil the f*cking party.' That c**t can't even f*cking sell out Apollo in Manchester – 3000 capacity in his own f*cking town, the f*cking embarrassing f*cking donut.

...I'd do a record, but listen, it depends on what kind of record it is. If it's anything like that sh*t he's putting out at the moment, I don't think anyone wants that. I think people would give you £100 million *not* to f*cking make that record, you know what I mean? They'd just go 'yeah, look, here's £100 million quid for the tour and here's another £100 million quid to not make a record like that.'

13 June: *Peter Crouch, Save Our Summer*, BBC

Liam

I'm ready to go me, man. Love is in the air... I think it's time, man, to get off the naughty step and stop sulking... I don't know how long it will last but... It's down to him, I think he's, er, I don't know what's going on in his world.

Opposite: *Noel Gallagher arriving at Wembley Stadium for the EURO 2020 Final on 11 July 2021 in London.*

28 November: *The Jonathan Ross Show, ITV*

Liam

When someone offers you a hundred million pounds to do a few gigs and that, man, you're gonna sort of go, 'Alright then, Yeah. There was a lot of money knocking about in there... it was a hundred million to do a tour and that and I'm thinking 'What?' I'm not a d*ckhead do you know what I mean? I'll have a bit of that.... He's not into it, is he?

...I think we're both the problem. And the problem is he thinks he's not the problem, he thinks I'm both the problems, whereas I'm just 'a' problem and he's a... I'm half the problem, whereas I can't be having him thinking that it's just that I'm the full problem... he needs to take on some of the problem.

2021

When... multiple variants of COVID-10 emerged... supporters of Donald Trump stormed Capitol Hill in Washington D.C. in an attempt to overturn the result of the 2020 United States presidential election... a container ship called *Ever Given* got caught in the Suez Canal and blocked the major international shipping route for six days... and Noel released his band's first greatest hits album, titled *Back the Way We Came: Vol. 1 (2011–2021)*.

No wonder the whole world and their mother were asking...

When are Oasis getting back together?

22 May: *The Jonathan Ross Show, ITV*

Noel

I find it a bit sad that there's a whole generation of kids, working-class kids, who have got nothing of their own to buy into and they're projecting all that onto a couple of 50-year-old fellas. Where's the new Oasis? Where's that?

...It was all wrapped up in youth and camaraderie and all that. Once that has gone you cannot put that genie back in the bottle. It would just be for showbiz and for a mere paltry £100 million!... There isn't £100million in the music business between all of us... if anybody wants to offer me £100million now, I'll say it now, I'll do it. I'll do it for £100million. Ludicrous. What is funny though is that I think Liam actually believes it.

29 April: *The Project, Australia*

Noel

People ask me that question on a daily basis and I can only say to you that I just don't feel like it. I don't feel like it. When you're in a band, it's an absolute compromise, so no I don't think I could come up with an idea and then run it by four people and then six weeks later, somebody knocks it back because their cat's got a cough, so y'know, I like to march to the beat of my own drum. Oasis is done I'm afraid.

…The legacy of the band is set in stone. If people have seen us, they'll understand what all the fuss is about. If you didn't see us, then that's tough cos I've never seen The Beatles or the Sex Pistols.

10 June: *Mr Porter, Net-a-Porter*

Noel

You don't really understand unless you've really been in it. Once you've quit, there is no going back. There's no point in going back.

11 June: *The Sun*

Noel

There are lots of things we have to agree to if anything is to happen. Most of them we don't agree on. Some we do. Even when someone says you need a name for this company, just to handle the business side of things, that's enough to give anybody the cold sweats. It's like, 'We've got to do a name now? Come up with a name everybody agrees on?' But Oasis never dies. It's daily emails and calls about Oasis.

12 June: *Manchester Evening News*

Noel

This might sound weird, but I'm actually proud that I left Oasis... and I'm proud that the band now is considered one of the greats when it wasn't in 2009.

...You'll be doing an interview for some f*cking regional paper in New Zealand when you're on tour, and they'll be asking you, 'Do you think Oasis will get back together?' And you just think, 'mate, do you think if Oasis was gonna do a reunion, we'd announce it in this f*cking magazine? No. Can we talk about something else?'

...I know people think it's some kind of elaborate f*cking plot to jack up the money, but you can't help those people. It gets a bit tedious but you know, I could choose to not answer the question and I don't, so it's kind of my own fault.

Liam performs at the Reading Festival on 29 August 2021 in the UK.

9 September: *How to Wow podcast with Chris Evans*

Noel
He's doing massive gigs, he's selling more records than I am and he's selling more tickets than I am, if you can believe that... So he's doing his thing and I'm doing mine and we're both pretty happy doing that at the moment... Liam's doing his thing, he's responsible for the legacy being what it is, he's keeping the flame alive and all that and good for him.

1 October: *Chris Moyles Show Radio X*

Chris Moyles rings up Liam live on air, and Liam pretends he thinks it's Noel.

Liam
Bonjour, is that you Noel? Is that you Noel? I knew you'd come round, I knew you'd come round. What's happening, what d'you want? You're not getting 50 million, mate.

2022

When... Russia invaded Ukraine, leading to economic sanctions and international condemnation... The Queen celebrated her Platinum Jubilee but died later in the year... Liz Truss lasted less than two months as the UK's prime minister... the world's population reached eight billion people... and Liam returned to play two huge solo concerts at Knebworth.

None of which stopped the lunatic hollering of...

When are Oasis getting back together?

4 February: *The Current Morning Show, Minnesota Public Radio*

Liam

He's started calling me by my first name now, so who knows? He's mentioning a lot of Oasis things. He might be sorry, or he might be getting soft in his old age. Who knows? I think it'd be better for him to do it, more than me.

12 February: *The Times*

Liam

He just seems like a different person. It's like he's been abducted. [The last time they met was at a Manchester City game.] He was there with his crew, I was with mine. We'd been drinking and he hadn't because he was on a health kick. I remember coughing and he shrank back... I thought, 'What the f*ck, man?'

...But you know I love him. We split up nearly 13 years ago. It's ridiculous. We can go on about whose fault it is, but he's his own man. If he really wanted to get in contact, for my mum's sake, he could do it, but he obviously doesn't want to. There are only so many olive branches you can offer.

28 April: *Esquire Magazine*

Liam

I like to think Oasis will get back together, but not this week... The door is ajar on everything. I wouldn't be surprised if space aliens landed tomorrow. I wouldn't be surprised if they were already here. I wouldn't be surprised if God walks among us. I wouldn't be surprised by all sorts.'

26 May: *The Guardian*

Liam

Would I like to reform Oasis with Noel Edmonds instead of Noel Gallagher? Maybe!

27 May: *Virgin Radio,*
Chris Evans' Breakfast Show with Sky, Virgin

Liam

I love him but he does my head in as well because we shouldn't have split up, and we should be making music. Do you know what I mean? And all that time wasted over just little bits and people go 'oh you slagged his missus off', he slagged mine, there was plenty of back and forth... so don't be making out it was just me... there's plenty of stories I could tell you mate, as well, do you know what I mean?

It's a shame that we split up because we should be making albums together. And rock'n'roll bands splitting up over, over, little bits of cr*p like that, sorry for swearing again, is pathetic... Y'know you split up because one of you dies or something... you don't split up because he said this and she said that. It's pathetic, innit?

29 May: *The Project, Australia*

Liam

So he's just being stubborn again... We'll have to wait and see. We should never have split up, y'know what I mean. He's the one sitting on the naughty step.

Noel and artists The Postman install a larger-than-life mural for Noel at his north London studio on 28 June 2022.

June: *Lad Bible*

Liam

I don't mind getting asked about that because it's natural, do you know what I mean? I like talking about Oasis because they were the best band in the world.

...Not this week but I'm ready to go. My bags are packed. Maybe the week after.

17 October: *Pub Talk podcast*

Noel

Er, would you go on holiday with your ex-missus?... As funny as this sounds, Oasis sell as many records now per year as we did when we were together. We're as popular now in the eyes of the people as we ever were. And I'm happy with it. If we got back together there would be a circus – and there's no point. Just leave it as it is. I'm happy. He's doing his thing. He's still selling out Knebworth. It's like, mate, good luck to you, do you know what I mean?'

2023

When... Israel invaded the Gaza strip as a response to the Hamas attacks in Israel on 7 October... the *Titan* submersible imploded while attempting to view the wreck of the *Titanic*... a high-altitude balloon moving through US airspace was suspected of being a Chinese spying device... and Noel reveals his latest album, *Council Skies*, is influenced by the end of his marriage.

So perhaps it wasn't quite so ridiculous to ask...

When are Oasis getting back together?

17 January: *Mike Sweeney, Radio Manchester*

Noel

Well one should never say never, right, but I have to be honest and for no other reason than, if Oasis hadn't fulfilled its potential, there'd be something left. Like the Stone Roses, when they came back, right, they didn't really fulfil their potential, right, so it was worthwhile for them to come back. Oasis smashed it repeatedly for twenty-odd years. It would have to take an extraordinary set of circumstances but that's not to say those circumstances wouldn't ever come about.

7 May: *The Irish Times*

Noel

...Some things are best left in the past, y'know? They just are. They. Just. Are. And I know we live in this modern world where the consumer gets what they want all the time; that's why the world is so sh*t.

23 May: *White and Jordan, talkSPORT*

Noel

He won't call me, I mean, he should call me because he's forever going on about it. You'd have thought by now he'd have some kind of plan... And if he's got a plan he should he should speak to me. He won't speak to me because he's a coward.

...But he should get some of his people, his agent, to call my people and say, 'Look, this is what we're thinking' and then we'll have a conversation about it... Until then, he's being a little bit disingenuous.

...I've always said that, y'know, things are best left in the past, but if he, if he... the thing with Liam is you read these things every day he's saying on his thing [Twitter], it's happening, it's happening, so he gets people's hopes up, right, all over the world. Then I get asked about it and I have to say, 'Well it's news to me' and I have to look like I'm dropping a big foot on it. Call me. Call me. Let's see what you've got to say... I'm open to a phone call... Other than that, stop playing with the kids, it's not fair on the fans.

25 May: *Spin*

***Noel is asked about reforming to tour and celebrate the upcoming 30th anniversary of* Definitely Maybe.**

Noel

I prefer to live in the moment and keep making new music. I acknowledge the past. *Definitely Maybe* is great and Oasis were great. It was an amazing moment in everybody's lives, but you've got one life. I don't intend to f*cking live it in the past.

...If Oasis hadn't fulfilled its potential, I might have a different attitude towards it. But as Oasis did everything it set out to do and more, I don't see the point.

Opposite: *Noel and High Flying Birds perform during South Facing 2023 at the Crystal Palace Bowl on 28 July in London.*

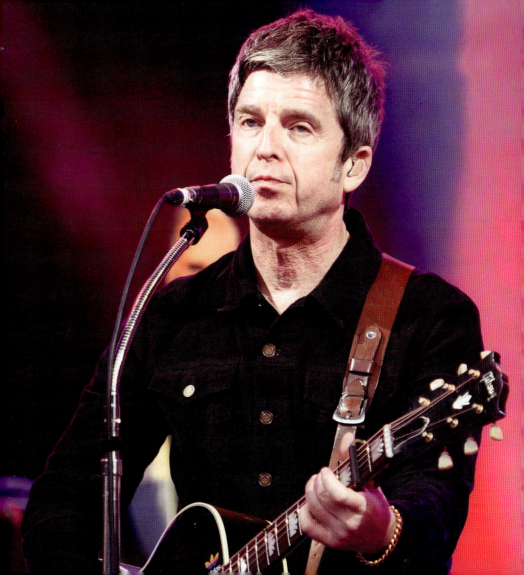

31 May: *The Sun, UK*

Noel

I get strangers coming up to me, saying, 'Be nice to your mum and get back together for her'. It's got nothing to do with my mum. I'm 56, not 17. She has never mentioned anything to me about it. She knows not to get involved. I wouldn't say to my mum, 'It's time you and Dad got back together'.

June: *Seattle station 98.9 KPNW*

Noel

Look, he's gonna have to call me. He's going to have to get somebody to call me, because he's been going on about it for the last f*cking 10 [years] or whatever it is and, you know, he doesn't want it. He knows that neither of us are particularly interested in it. I know he doesn't want it. I'm very comfortable with what I'm doing. I couldn't give a flying f*ck one way or the other, but he keeps going on about it and I'm like, 'OK, well, f*cking call us then. Let's see what you've got to say,'... You've made up all these imaginary ground rules over the years and told kids, 'It's happening. It's happening now. It's coming. It's definitely happening.' Blah blah blah. I dare him.

(*Noel addresses camera*) 'I f*cking dare you to call me. I dare you to call me. And you won't call me, because if you do call me and I go, 'Actually that's a good idea. Actually, that might work', then the a*se falls out of his trousers, because then you've got to be in the same room as me and we both know how that ends up. So you call me. Stop tweeting. You're bigger than that. You're better than that.

1 June: *Johnny Vaughan Show, Radio X*

Johnny Vaughan recalls the £8 million in an Adidas bag offer they joked about four years previously.

Noel

I would consider it. I would properly consider it. It used to really annoy me when I first started and now it's just… It's just whatever really.

…I'm fascinated with people asking the same question and getting the same answer, but the thing that's really ongoing and will never get old is how the music just keeps appealing to another generation of fans.

2 June: *The Times*

Noel

Liam ain't called... I'm not expecting him to, because he's full of sh*t and very disingenuous with his beloved Oasis fans. I say to him, 'Get somebody to call somebody my end. Let's see what you've got to say.' Guess what? My phone has not twitched once.

...If it's going to happen, Liam has to pull it off. It's got to be the best it has ever been. But he's one of these guys and they're ten a penny, particularly up in Manchester, the bully, who when you put it on 'em and say, 'Come on then, let's see what you've got,' start doing a lot of harrumphing.

...Liam is like a violent version of Arthur Fonzarelli [The Fonze]. So I'll say it again: I'm free, back end of 2024. He could even video himself calling me. That would be good for his little f*cking Twitter feed. But since then he's gone quiet. Funny, innit?

3 June: *NME*

Andrew Trendell asks Noel if it feels odd to be on the road at the same time as the reunion tours of Oasis' old Britpop peers, Blur and Pulp.

Noel

I didn't know that, but good luck to them! Blur never split up, did they? Pulp never split up, they just went and did other things, which is the adult way of doing it. Sadly, my f*cking band were very far from adult about it. It was a bit more crash and burn.

...There's never really been a serious offer about 'The Big O' getting back together, but there you go.

5 June: *2FM with Dave Fanning, RTE*

Noel

You become institutionalised by a band, the way it's just all that you know. All that you know is playing *(What's the Story) Morning Glory?* and 'Cigarettes & Alcohol' and it becomes second nature. And when it becomes second nature, it becomes boring.

...It could easily easily easily be done again but... no one's ever been offered [£100 million] but Liam believes in the Tooth Fairy and the Loch Ness Monster. So I'm afraid he's not a very reliable witness. It would have to take an extraordinary chain of events for it to happen. I'm not saying [that] chain of events could or would never happen. I just don't see it. Our kid can be very disingenuous with the way he keeps saying to people on Twitter 'It's happening. It's happening. It's happening'.

6 June: *Table Manners with Jessie and Lennie Ware*

Noel

But I've got extremely fond memories of the Oasis thing and all that but it would have to take an extraordinary chain of events for it to happen again

15 June: *Jo Whiley, Brit Pop Legends, BBC Radio 2*

Liam

Our kid's been called many times to get the band back together. It just so happens that this time he wants it when he's got an album out... The way I see it is, it ain't happening. I won't be calling him, he'll be calling me. He split the band up on *his* terms and I'll be getting it back together on *my* terms. And I'm a reasonable person but I'm very good friends with the universe and we have ways of making it happen 'cos it will come round to him calling me... I don't sit there going 'it's gonna happen next week trust me', like that. I think it will happen...

(Jo plays in Noel's 'I dare you to call me' clip from Noel's KPNW interview a few days earlier.)

...Ha ha! Is this where he turns into the wrestler Rick Flair? 'I dare you, I dare you.' I've seen it, I don't want to hear it again because it will put me in a bad mood...

(Jo stops playing Noel's address to Liam and goes on to ask how hard it must be for Peggy with battling sons.)

She's kind of over it, y'know what I mean, she's like not bothered. She's just like, we're a pair of idiots... The olive branch has been put out to him many a time... I haven't personally called him... I haven't got his number...

...It would be lovely for brothers to be talking and me mam and all that and my other brother and families that haven't seen each other, like my kids haven't seen his kids I haven't seen his kids. So all that would be great and then we could get back to business.

(Jo: Maybe you could solve this if you simply just went, 'Do you know what, I'm going to – I'm going to call him'.)

Have you got his number?... Go on then let's call him now... don't be silly I'm not doing it. I'm not giving it to you just yet. We'll move on, yeah?

25 August: *The Sun*

Noel

It's funny — we are all at a certain age now, my hair was a bit thicker in Oasis. We'd have to see what everyone's hair was looking like.

9 October: *Take Five, ABC Australia*

Noel

You get one shot at life, why be unhappy?... There's not a day goes by that I don't , y'know, that I don't think f*cking hell we did something really spectacular there. I still can't articulate what it was, d'you know what I mean, because it was more, although it was the songs and all that, it was more than that though, it was more than that.

2024

When... the Labour Party won the UK election for the first time in a generation, resulting in Sir Keir Starmer becoming prime minister... Julian Assange left the UK after being freed from prison... the Francis Scott Key Bridge in Baltimore collapsed when it was hit by a container ship... and Liam teamed up with his hero, the ex-Stone Roses guitarist John Squire, to release a collaborative album.

Little did humanity know, it only had a few months left to ask...

When are Oasis getting back together?

10 January: *The Guardian*

Liam
I haven't seen him, and we won't see each other.

24 February: *The Sunday Times*

Liam

He knows I'm not going to call him. He's the one who split the band up, so he'll be doing the calling, and if there is no calling, we won't be getting back together. To be fair, though, I can see it happening. Now things have changed in his personal life, I can see him looking back, not looking back in anger, and going, 'Do you know what? I was really mean to my little brother. Now it is time for me to send him a box of chocolates.'

Oh, without a doubt. I love my brother, I love my family, and all that Oasis sh*t, there was no need for it, you know what I mean?... I don't hold grudges, man, and if Oasis got back together it would be great because I would only have to sing 15 songs and he could do the rest. I could do that standing on me head.

That was my band and that was all I knew. I lived and breathed it, so once it was gone I was like, who the f*ck am I, really? Everyone knows me as that guy from Oasis. If that's not there anymore, I'm just a hollow f*cking wandering dude from the Nineties. But you move on. Life is just one big conveyor belt, innit?

15 February: *Mojo Magazine*

Liam

I did call him! Well, my people called Noel's management team. We put an offer on the table for an Oasis thing – because we got offered it – and he said no. It was a big tour, a lot of money. He turned it down. I get it, he's got a divorce going down. I'll do the *Definitely Maybe* thing… [the 30th anniversary tour of *Definitely Maybe*] …and have a nice time without him… It's down to the universe. It'll happen when it happens, it's not in our hands anymore. Me, I love nostalgia though. I'm doing the lot. Every album, even… what was the last one?

2 March: *The Independent*

Liam

Haven't seen him for ages, man… but I think he was at me mam's the other weekend. He seems to be doing well, man. Seems to be a lot happier in his skin. Surprise sur-f*cking-prise… All my f*cking olive branches have gone. I've got none left.

3 March: *Manchester Evening News*

Liam
I'm not fed up, but everyone else seems to be. But it isn't happening. It isn't happening this week anyway.

9 April: *NME*

Liam
Noel's still a c**t!... it's not happening, mate.

18 April: *Hunger Magazine*

Liam
I don't think we need it, but I know people would like to see it.

Before a reunion, I think that me and our kid need to sort of be brothers again, because it's been too long now... I'm ready to go. I'm still cool, I can do the songs. I've proved to everyone that I'm not a f*cking lazy a*se and that was Noel's thing [about me] – 'Well, he's lazy and he's this and he's that.' I'm ready to go. So, if it happens, it happens.

May: *The Jonathan Ross Show, ITV*

Liam

I haven't spoken to him. I haven't spoken to him, I haven't spoken to him for about ten years – 2009, I think... (*Audience SIGHS*). Don't start that. No, I'm having a great time. Don't worry about it. It's all good man... That's a 'no'... Not this week, 'no'.

3 June:

Liam introducing 'Half the World Away' at Utilita Arena, Cardiff on the *Definitely Maybe* 30th anniversary tour.

Liam

So, I'm going to dedicate this next tune to my little brother, who's still playing hard to get. But that's all right. But word on the street is he was spotted in a really posh chocolate shop, one of them Thorntons, buying some chocolates. So you never know! You know what I mean?

1 August:

Noel joshes with a heckler at a High Flying Birds concert at the Halifax Piece Hall

Noel

What is happening with Liam next year? I don't know. You tell me... Why? Is something going on? Is there?

Lazio fans respond to the news of Oasis' reunion during the Serie A football match between SS Lazio and AC Milan.

27 August: *Statement from Oasis*

The guns have fallen silent.
The stars have aligned.
The great wait is over.

August: *YouTube*

(A group of small children bump into Noel in a shop and ask him why he fell out with Liam.)

Noel
'Cause he stole my teddy bear... Not lying. He stole it in 1978.

7 September:

Liam tweets that he no longer thinks Noel is a potato.

EPILOGUE

Nineteen eighty-two, Burnage: a ten-year-old Liam is berating a guitar-noodling teenage Noel for not playing football with him. Peggy Gallagher shakes her head and tells them both to shut up. Jump forward a few decades and the dynamics are pretty much the same, except Liam and Noel are arguing via the world's media about Noel refusing to do a hundred-million-pound world tour.

When are Oasis getting back together? *That* is the question. And sometimes the answers to *that* question are so playful they make us feel that we're eavesdropping on two brothers joyfully ribbing each other. At other times, their answers are so personal and vicious we feel we should stop paying attention... but we just can't. As Liam puts it, it's... 'very complicated. I wouldn't wish it on anyone but it's fun as well.'

Reviewing Liam and Noel's reponses, it's interesting to examine the various themes and phrases that have keep popping up. Liam relentlessly stated that Noel's walking out on Oasis in 2009 was a preplanned strategy to launch his solo career, rather than a spontaneous act born of frustration. Meanwhile, Noel repeatedly asserted that Liam was so erratic on tour, he couldn't rely on him to finish a gig and that's why the Big 'O' couldn't reform. But as we get closer to the announcement of the reunion, Noel ruminates that Liam's unpredictability and volatility was what excited the public. Liam tells us a thousand times that he's 'out of olive branches' and his 'bags are packed', while Noel increasingly uses 'Never say never' and

A mural depicting Liam and Noel Gallagher, by artist Snow Graffiti appears on a wall at the Coach and Horses pub in Whitefield, Manchester.

'I just can't see it', when he's clearly starting to see 'it' more and more clearly.

Liam is erratic but he's also remarkably consistent. He said incessantly, for 15 years, he'd like to get the band back together. However, he would also start an answer to the reunion question with 'I believe Oasis will sail again and it'll be glorious', and end it with 'D'you think I want to be in a band with that c**t?'

Noel, too, blew hot and cold throughout the Oasis interregnum. Often, he rebutted the query with a steadfast 'No'. Then, at other times, he's suggest everything rests on the vagaries of male pattern baldness.

Although, even with a reconciliation on the horizon, the brothers were still as aggy as ever. The hilariously childish statements they both put forward as to who was going to telephone whom as the reunion loomd is like a satire of the lovey-dovey 'You put the phone down', 'No, you put the phone down'. But more 'You pick up the phone, you pr*ck', 'No you pick up the phone, you tw*t!' (BTW: after the reunion announcement, Liam tweeted that he called Noel first but jokingly asked his followers not to tell anyone as he didn't want to look 'soft'.)

What lessons can be learned from this book? That there's power in patience, persistence and never letting go of the dream. And, if you want someone to do something, just keep calling them a c**t.

PICTURE CREDITS

All images © Getty Images